Juli Carson
The Hermeneutic Impulse

Aesthetics of an Untethered Past

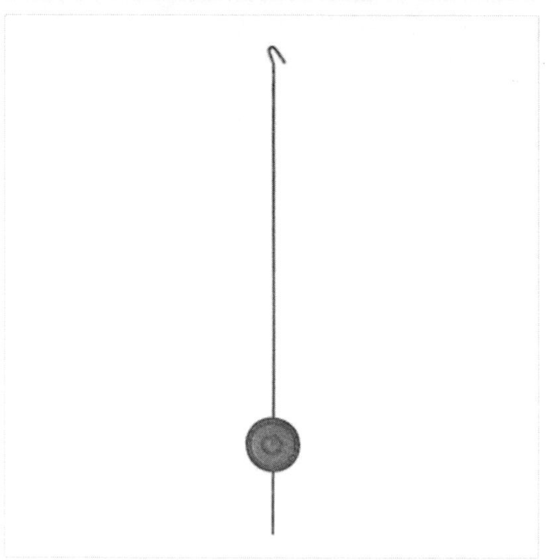

Pendel

3,95 €

inkl. 19 % USt zzgl. Versandkosten

Pendulum, screenshot from the web page of online seller www.selva.de. Collage: Michael Dreyer

Juli Carson
The Hermeneutic Impulse

Aesthetics of an
Untethered Past

b_books · Reihe PoLYpeN

Attribution

The essays collected in this volume were written inter-textually while residing in three cities, immediately preceding and following the election of Donald J. Trump to the office of U.S. President. "After *After Before*" was written in New York City during the "American Summer" of 2016, while "Aesthetics of an Untethered Past" and "Schmitt, You and Me" were written in Irvine, California, during Trump's first year in office, against the backdrop of the white nationalist riot now known simply as "Charlottesville." Meanwhile, the volume's bookends, "Parallax Imaginary – Between Two (Event) Horizons, the Artwork" and "Afterword: Myself as Another," were written on the eve of the 2018 midterm elections – a referendum on Trump's presidency – while I was the Philippe Jabre Professor in Art History and Curating at the American University in Beirut. Accordingly, certain themes, events and *mise-en-scènes* repeat – traumatically, but meaningfully – throughout the volume's three case study artworks. Finally, "Looking Back: That Obscure Object of Gender," written in 2013, comprises an appendix whose anamorphic situatedness places us (at once) then *there*, when our current historical crisis still lay on the horizon, and here *now*, when issues of gender couldn't be more imperative.

Contents

Parallax Imaginary
Between Two (Event) Horizons,
the Artwork[1]

If we define the task of hermeneutics as the bridging of personal or historical distance between minds, then the experience of art would seem to fall entirely outside its province. For of all the things that confront us in nature and history, it is the work of art that speaks to us most directly. It possesses a mysterious intimacy that grips our entire being, as if there were no distance at all between us and the work, and every encounter with it is an encounter with ourselves [...]. In fact, an absolute contemporaneousness exists between the work and its present beholder that persists unhampered despite every intensification of the historical consciousness. The reality of the work of art and its expressive power cannot [therefore] be restricted to its original historical horizon, in which its beholder actually seems to become the contemporary of the creator. It seems instead to belong to the experience of art that the work of art always has its own present.[2]
    Hans-Georg Gadamer

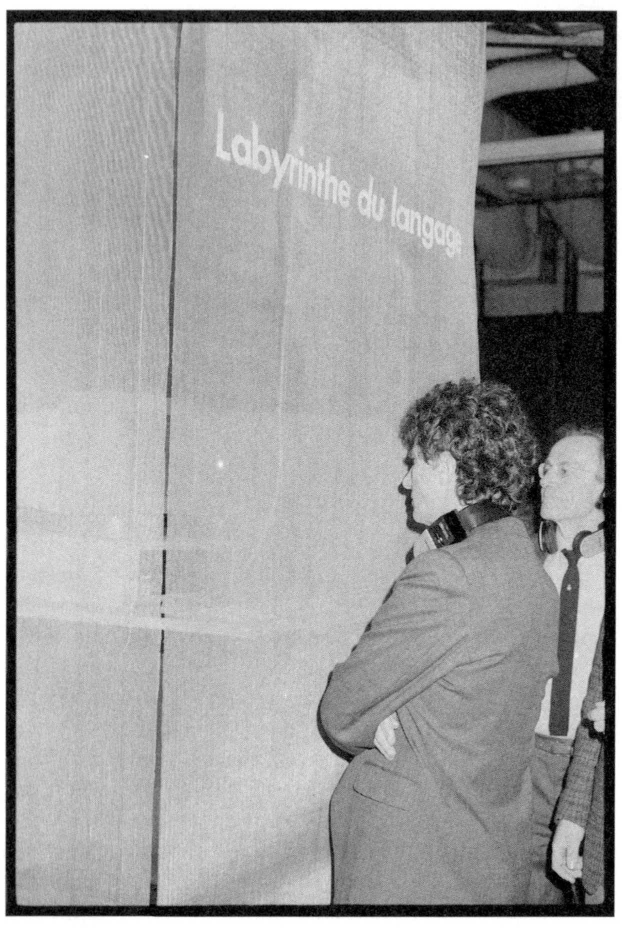

Jack Lang, Jean-François Lyotard, opening reception,
Les Immatériaux, Centre Pompidou, March 27, 1985

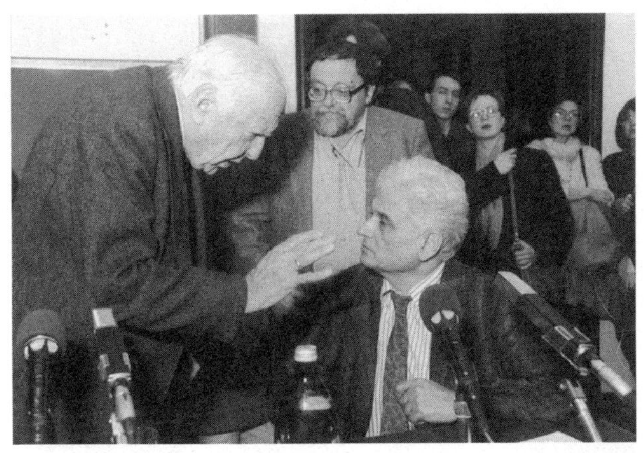

Hans-Georg Gadamer and Jacques Derrida,
Heidelberg Conference, 1988

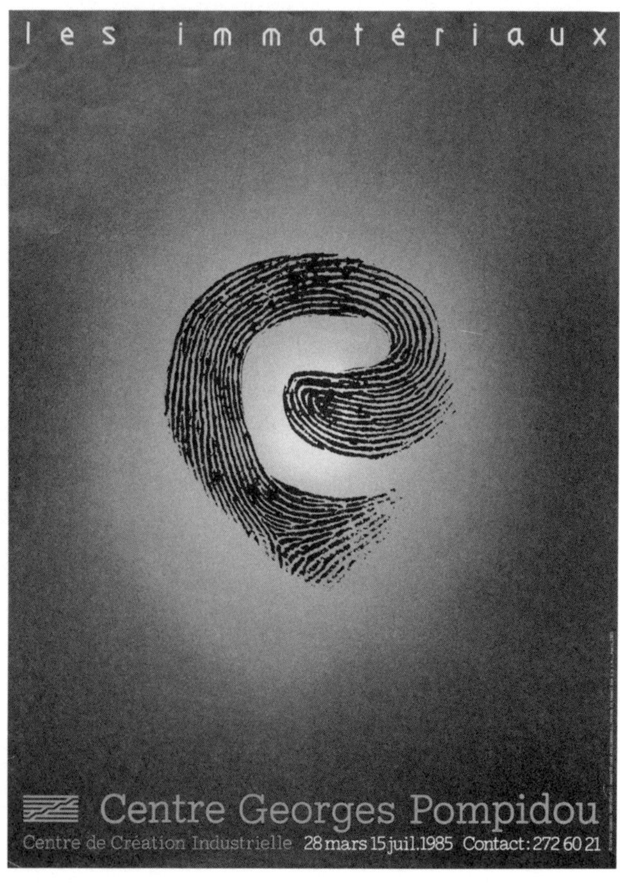

Les Immatériaux Exhibition Poster. Design by Luc Maillet,
Grafibus, 1985

Primal Scene(s)

My interest in *post*-hermeneutics – "post" in the sense of a "post-structuralism" that enacts a deconstruction, not a negation – is inspired by two events I know only through secondary written accounts. One is curatorial; the other philosophical. Interpolated between them is the crisis of historical consciousness. Looking back now on the moment of my primary encounter with each of these events – their secondary discursive transposition *constituting* my primary encounter with them – I see that each impacted me just as Gadamer describes one's experience with a work of art. In his terms, these encounters possessed "a mysterious intimacy" that "gripped me" as if there were no distance at all between me and the prior event I was experiencing second hand. Further, my encounter with these events was an encounter with myself: a subject at once historically and contemporarily sited within them.

First, the curatorial event.

It was 1988, one year after the great Stock Market Crash that gave us "Black Monday" on October 19, and one year before the fall of the Berlin Wall on November 9. In a graduate seminar on postmodernity, I recall my professor introducing a "transgressive" exhibition, *Les Immatériaux*, that French philosopher Jean-François Lyotard had recently curated at the Centre Pompidou in 1985. If I say, then, that *Les Immatériaux* "happened" to me in 1988, it's simply because it was there and then that I experienced the 1985 exhibition by way of John Rajchman's review "The Postmodern Museum" as a contemporaneous event.[3] Recalling this some thirty years later, what strikes me as even more uncanny is that the year 1988 is the eve of what was to be *Les Immatériaux's* anterior future. It marks *what will have been* after the fall of the Berlin

Wall, which no one saw coming in 1985, nor did I in 1988. But I'm racing ahead. Back to the event.

In his dual capacity as philosopher and co-curator of *Les Immatériaux*, Lyotard's question was the following: How does one organize into representation the sublime subject of late-stage capitalism,[4] one that is "authentically" unrepresentable precisely because it has the veiled characteristic of the unconscious and the pulsatile nature of what Jacques Lacan called the ever elusive Real? For just as this *thing* – this subject of capitalism – surfaces within language, it is subsumed into Symbolic convention. Subsequently, capitalism's quintessential sublimity, its *great ephemeral skin* – as Lyotard characterized it in his self-described "evil little book" *Libidinal Economy* – is shed off, sliding back into nothingness. And yet, it was this sublime subject, more specifically this *postmodern* sublime subject, that *Les Immatériaux* set out to "demonstrate" rather than "represent." This was *Les Immatériaux*'s fundamental quagmire because the sublime takes place only …

"[…] when the imagination fails to present an object which might, if only in principle, come to match a concept. We have the Idea of the world (the totality of what it is), but we do not have the capacity to show an example of it. We have the Idea of the simple (that which cannot be broken down, decomposed), but we cannot illustrate it with a sensible object which would be a 'case' of it. We can conceive the infinitely great, the infinitely powerful, but every presentation of an object destined to 'make visible' this absolute greatness or power appears to us painfully inadequate."[5]

As for *Les Immatériaux's* content – our collective consciousness of late-stage capitalism, aesthetically, technologically and philosophically – this quagmire intensifies. Although we may be able to conceive of multinational corporations, globalized markets, labor, mass consumption and liquid multinational flows of capital, how do we *picture* this, psychically? How do we wrap our heads around it? According to Lyotard, it's precisely that impasse – the contradiction between our intuitive and rational faculties – that needs to be revealed in all its perplexity, and certainly at the expense of being dialectically resolved. Such that, for Lyotard, it's better to grasp capitalism *as* the sublime – to encounter this impasse willfully – than it is to cognitively map capital's reification through a positivist language of Symbolic unity, as someone like Lyotard's interlocutor Fredric Jameson might have it. Indeed, it was this impasse – reified by the labyrinthic nature of Lyotard's installation evoking Jorge Luis Borges' "The Library of Babel" – that marked *Les Immatériaux* as at once misconstrued and destined to the canon. During the exhibition's run – amidst the public's aporic attraction and repulsion to it – Lyotard melancholically lamented: "That we know not how to name what awaits us is a sure sign that it awaits us."[6] It would seem that embracing the sublime nature of capitalism entailed the concomitant encounter with the sublimity of time itself.

Indeed, looking back at *Les Immatériaux* today, it seems the exhibition's anticipated anterior-future has come to pass. Or – as John Rajchman recently reflected – *Les Immatériaux* was "a pre-1989 event that foresaw the advent of globalization and accelerated exchange."[7] Accordingly, while *Les Immatériaux* pointedly asked: "What would this postmodern condition *be*?", Lyotard did not know at the time what the future held, only that it held him waiting. With *Les Immatériaux's* postmodern *mise-en-scène* now on the horizon behind us, it's *our* future that holds us in its waiting, precisely as we circle back to key 20th century debates that, in 1988, on the eve of the end of the Cold War's great partition, we thought were long gone. These were, and still are, confounding questions. As Freud famously put it: *Wo Es war, soll Ich werden.*

What gripped me then about *Les Immatériaux* was that curatorial practice, a convention deeply embedded within capital, could be connected to philosophy the way the "New Art History" had been connected to critical theory. Meaning, one could actually theorize and/or philosophize a given subject through the performative gesture of "curating as a verb," as I've recently come to define a modality of this practice.[8] What grips me now is how the recollection of this event occasions the embodied performative instance of *seeing oneself as a deferred subject* within history, the hermeneutic phenomenon by which *my encounter with the event is simultaneously an encounter with myself.* This kind of phenomenological hermeneutics – what was coined "new historicism" in the 1980s – does *not* instance an (unrevealed) narcissistic drive. Rather, I would argue, it potentially detaches conventional historicism from its Archimedean point and reconnects it to an ethical, culpable encounter with the observing self. From that vantage, the self-reflective chain of encounters I describe – my 2018 encounter with my 1988 encounter with 1985 – leaves me wondering why, in turn, I have no memories of the height of the civil war in Beirut, concurrent with *Les Immatériaux.* I ask that question now because Beirut is the city in which these memories have most recently resurfaced or re-emerged. Accordingly, I am driven to perform a Gramscian kind of "inventory of the self," in situ, through which I now recall the (my) Eurocentric Archimedean point through which an American gaze of the Middle East, in 1988, repetitively screened, as a totality, the fog of the Arab Cold War. Political memory – the essence of which is always anomia – thus demands a speculative approach to positing collective historical memory, one that is willfully aporic vis-à-vis the Archimedean approach to historical representation. When setting out to make theory in a museum, or otherwise, this speculative approach must be mindfully engaged *repetitively.*

Which brings us to the second event.

In 2016 I discovered quite accidentally, *as if by chance* – knowing full well that in Lacanese there are no accidents – a volume Fordham Press had just published entitled *Heidegger, Philosophy and Politics: The Heidelberg Conference*. As Reiner Wiehl's preface recounts, it was "a trace of a memorable discussion" that took place on the evening of February 5, 1988, at the University of Heidelberg between Jacques Derrida, Hans-Georg Gadamer, and Philippe Lacoue-Labarthe on the subject of Heidegger's dubious entanglement with the Third Reich.[9] Jean-Luc Nancy's forward further recalls that the original French volume – *La conférence de Heidelberg (1988): Heidegger, Portée philosophique et politique de sa pensée* – had been published two years prior, the same year that Heidegger's *Schwarze Hefte* were also published. These were, memorably, the personal notebooks that had ostensibly exposed the philosopher's more willful anti-Semitism. But at their core laid a riddle. It was strange enough that these personal sentiments contradicted Heidegger's published sentiments, stranger still that Heidegger himself had intended that the notebooks be published posthumously.

In 2014 a *demand* was thus made of the as yet unpublished Heidelberg Conference. Or rather, the event that took place in Heidelberg twenty-six years prior begged its own transcription, which is to say its own repetition. This was easy enough to do, as Calle-Gruber recalls, as the conference had been so highly mediated, a mediation further redoubled in transcribing the French and English volumes:

"The event took place: it was a great moment of explication (Auseinandersetzung) and of truth(s) between Hans-Georg Gadamer, Jacques Derrida, and Philippe Lacoue-Labarthe. It was transmitted, recorded, photographed, filmed by television (Westdeutscher Rundfunk), and commented on by special correspondents from numerous papers. Then retranscribed, corrected by each of the participants, reread by Derrida, whom Gadamer had asked to review his own interventions. The text of the public debate, and of the meeting with journalists the following day was ready. But we all agreed, all of us, to defer publication: to wait for tensions to subside, along with the noise of the media's uncontrollable effects."

Needless to say, in 1988 the conference had been thoroughly *worked through*, but not meaningfully transferred into discourse. It would only be repeated twenty-six years later, first in French – when a demand was made by the posthumous Heidegger – and then in English, when I happened upon this very demand in the course of tracing the concept of "double-mimesis." More on that momentarily. First, a few words on the subject of transference and repetition, according to Lacan, may be helpful.

Because repetition is bound up with transference – transference entails the subject's self-deception that his or her conscious desire for the Other spontaneously originates, for the first time, within him or herself – Lacan asserts that it's the subject's *unconscious* that surfaces in the field of the Other. Which is to say that while desire may be felt as one's own as a primordial self-deception, in reality this deception is the sublimation of the subject's repressed knowledge that one's desire is the desire of the Other. Accordingly, transference entails the repetition of a demand addressed to the field of any given contemporary Other, which, in fact, is the unconscious return of a *past* demand addressed to an historical Other in a completely different scenario. As Philippe Julien explains: "Because the demand was not previously recognized, it returns in unconscious formations (symptoms, dreams, parapraxes, jokes). Thus, as soon as one subject addresses another subject in full, authentic speech, there is transference, such that recognition occurs at the very point where before there had been none: a blank page, a censored chapter, a rejected (*verworfen*) fragment from history."[10]

Back to the conference.

In 1988 Heidegger's specter appeared as the haunting Other for a series of desiring subjects, each of whom had their own conflicting terms of transference laid upon them, which is to say, each of whom were determined by their own unconscious pulsations. On this note, the conference's primary players, Derrida and Gadamer, transferred two distinct phantasmatic Oedipal *mise-en-scènes* of their philosopher Father (figure), based on the fact that while Derrida was a student *of* Heidegger, Gadamer was Heidegger's *actual* protégé. Correspondingly, the conference produced a kind of surplus value – one exceeding the symbolic order they had hoped to produce – by conjuring up the Father's phantom vis-à-vis the philosopher's repressed political past. In the course of Derrida and Gadamer's back and forth, "two Heideggers" surfaced. One was a "Hermeneutical Heidegger," born of Gadamer's desire to commune with the past, and the other was a "Deconstructive Heidegger," born of Derrida's propensity for endless deferral. What the *Heidelberg Conference* therefore revealed was the manner in which these interlocutors' respective positions – on the subject of historical consciousness – were inextricably intertwined, rather than opposed (metaphorically), no less so than the life and death drives themselves are intertwined. The performative nature of it all, characterized by the tenacious working-through of the conference by its participants – the taping, photographing, reviewing, writing and rewriting, followed by the *waiting* and eventual posthumous publication for both Derrida and Gadamer – was precisely what gripped me.

To hold *The Heidelberg Conference* volume in my hands, to flip studiously through its pages in the summer of 2016, was thus to encounter a temporal loop of conflicting desires for historical agency and accountability. In the course of "witnessing" the participants' individual transference upon the many Heideggers haunting the conference – by way of my own transference onto each one of them – what surfaced was thus the simultaneous repression and repetition of various primal scenes. For one, the 1987 Klaus Barbie trial had, at that time, recently exposed the extent of France's insidious anti-Semitism, a politically repressed fact of the Vichy regime. In the same year Victor Farías's *Heidegger and Nazism* (although widely disputed as simplistic) exposed Heidegger's own complicity with the Third Reich. These were just two repressed realities that returned on that evening of February 5, 1988, at the University of Heidelberg.

Flash forward to the recent past.

If the publishing of Heidegger's *Schwarze Hefte* in 2014 prompted the posthumous return of Derrida and Gadamer's dialogue, in an uncanny way the English translation of this same volume, which surfaced in 2016, corresponds to what I'm calling the "American Summer," the series of manipulated media events that brought us the catastrophic election (in the minds of progressives and moderates) of Donald J. Trump to the office of U.S. president. And that's where the self-inventory of historical memory vis-à-vis the return of a repressed past, in the guise of a secondary reception, comes up again. As two moments collapse onto one other, as two moments repeat through their conjoined echo chambers, the realization surfaces to us now that Trump is both symptom and cause of what has long been repressed within the so-called American Dream. The repressed reality of that dream is what the dream's manifest content covers over: that at the bottom of any and all semblance of a post-race American "exceptionalism" – still a functioning myth for many – lies a pernicious racism, the toxic remains of the nation's traumatic founding on the backs of slaves. In all of this – the collapse of 1987/1988 with 2014/2016 – I encountered myself as a subject of history, as contemporaneous with these historical events, traumatic or otherwise, inasmuch as they were contemporaneous with me.

This post-hermeneutic moment thus affords two sets of parallax imaginaries, each at play with the other, in which 1988 acts as the subtending hinge. In one imaginary – that of *Les Immatériaux* – 1988 is the deferred moment from which I can recall gazing back onto 1985. Yet it's also a moment when I recall looking forward, in anticipation, to "what will have been" in the events of 1989. In the other imaginary – that of the *Heidelberg Conference* – 1988 is at once the actual scene of an event that would be deferred into transcription twenty-six years later, roughly the time of this writing. But it's also the secondary site for the conference's participants to gaze back upon their own primal scene: the events of World War II. In one imaginary, a personal recollection is embedded within the historical field. In the other, the historical field is embedded within a personal reception.

Cutting across this moebius strip of the personal-historical – in which 1930s totalitarianism is hinged by the year 1988 onto the repetition of both moments in the contemporary milieu of 2016 – is a rupture that was formerly presumed to have taken place in the transitional moment of 1989, which, of course, did not happen. I'm speaking again of the so-called collapse of communism and the triumph of globalized post-party, post-regional politics, otherwise known as "neoliberal economics." Yes, neoliberalism has thrived, though at the expense of being both cause and symptom of a destructive, populist global neo-authoritarianism. At the same time, 1989 also marked the height of the American Culture Wars, something progressives of my generation thought we had finally won in 2008 and 2012, given the election of the first African-American president followed by marriage equality, two monumental victories in the field of identity politics. Again, we were wrong. In retrospect, for writers and artists of my generation, 1989 wasn't a rupture. From one perspective, it's a primary scene of trauma, from another, it's the stuff of Greek tragedy. In both cases, it's a matter of tenacious, insistent (unconscious) repetition.

Which brings us, one last time, back to Freud.

If repetition is a transference of the forgotten past onto the present, then the compulsion to repeat replaces the impulse to remember.[11] In the language of psychoanalysis, this defines transference *neurosis*. But there is another route. *Meaningful* transference replaces transference neurosis when repetition is neither repressed from our consciousness nor indulged, when we *persevere* through repetition in a self-aware manner. In the analytic scenario, the analyst – a mirror of the analysand in Lacan's terms – provides the non-explanatory guidance necessary for the analysand's gradual self-awareness. In the cultural milieu the artist/writer – a double mimesis in Gadamer's terms – provides the non-didactic aesthetic production necessary for a corresponding new historicist memory. I'm therefore conjecturing a post-structuralist hermeneutics – a hermeneutic *impulse,* actually – that would then play with the horizon between an historicist interpretation of contemporary art and a contemporary interpretation of historical events. Within this postulation, the artwork might performatively take up the space that the year 1988 did in my anecdotal history, which is to say that it might fill the gap of the missing chapter masked by the parallax points of view of any given event lying upon our collective historical horizon. Analogously, the artwork might then expose something personal within the historical: the nature of the subject's chiastic drives – one to repeat unconsciously, the other to repress consciously. Left unexposed, the reality of this entwined operation inherent to both parallax vision and the drives is a road block en route to any collective, historical anamnesis of which post-hermeneutics might speak. Instead, should the artwork meaningfully interpolate that forgotten chapter *as* a gap, it might then (re)produce that gap by way of repeating it, true, but repeating as something to consider, paradoxically, as a *thing* we might view and contemplate.

What follows are three case studies of artworks that initiate this interpolative act.

After *After Before*

[If] communism can no longer be the unsurpassable horizon of our time [it's] not because we have passed beyond any horizon [...]. The ultimate limit of community traces an entirely different line.[12]
    Jean-Luc Nancy

That we know not how to name what awaits us is the sure sign that it awaits us.[13]
    Jean-François Lyotard

We hear it all the time. That name denoting an absolute, sovereign citizenry: *community*. The "black community," the "Jewish community," the "gay community," but where are these homogenous entities? Pollsters and sociologists make a living calculating their communal desire through *demographics*, but it's increasingly hard to identify communities with any cohesion – aesthetically, philosophically or politically – aside from the contingent voting blocs they collectively form when the "public sphere" threatens expulsion. If the word "community" is ultimately a sign of *itself*, then perhaps it's an indication that community *has yet to be*, something we continuously aim at establishing. A good simile is the horizon. When you approach it, the horizon is both fixed and *not* fixed, receding at the same distance from you based upon the location of your own perspective. And yet, community is nothing like the horizon. Although it's visually deceiving, the horizon is quite real and mathematically calculable. But a community – one based upon a political program or absolute ideal – is really nothing *but* a mirage. As Jean-Luc Nancy argues, throughout time, communities have been nostalgically conceived upon a *lost* commune, a phantasmatic "horizon" *behind* us. It's a communal-ideal we've been chasing ever since Plato kicked the artists out of his Republic, the Christians created their brotherhoods, and Rousseau penned his *Social Contract* in service of Enlightenment *fraternité*. Even Guy Debord's *Situationist International* falls in line with this thinking, his renowned *Society of the Spectacle* being no less conceived upon a communal model of lost immanence than were his predecessors' treatises. And, so it follows, from Nancy's point of view, what these communities have *really* lost "is lost only in the sense that such 'loss' is constitutive of 'community' itself."[14] Hence the horizon – that communal-ideal predicated on collective desire for a perceived loss – that lay *before* Sharon Hayes's experimental documentary, *After Before*. Question is, does Hayes chase it or interrogate it?

Fast forward to the year 2004.

The world is tumultuously unstable, something we haven't yet adjusted to after 9/11. The CIA admits there were no weapons of mass destruction used to justify the U.S. invasion of Iraq; terrorists bomb four rush-hour trains in Madrid, killing

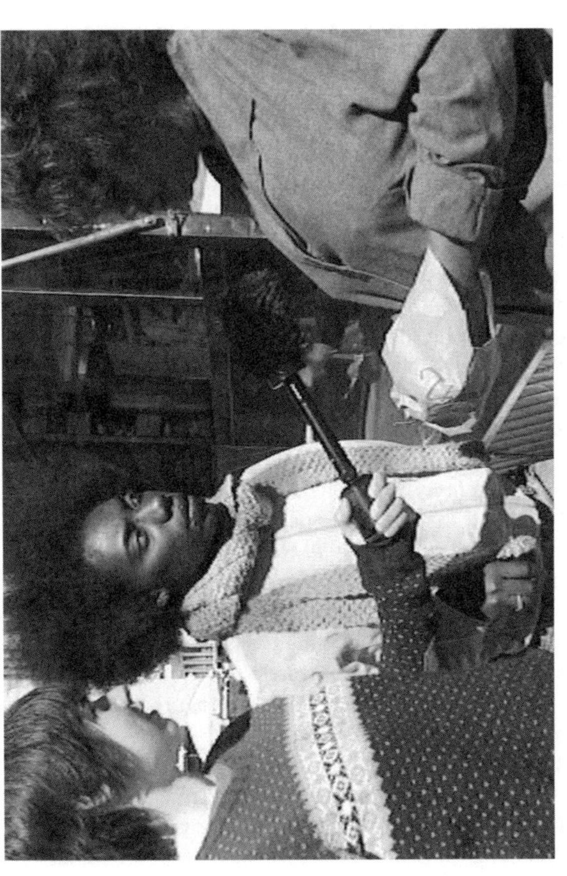

Sharon Hayes, "After Before", 2005, Performers: Kemba Bloodworth and Ewa Einhorn, video still

191 people; Chechen president Akhmad Kadyrov is assassinated; Nick Berg, an American civilian contractor in Iraq, is decapitated by al-Qaeda-linked terrorists who web-distribute the video; hearings begin in Iraq in the trial of former president Saddam Hussein; the Orange Revolution begins in the Ukraine; a 9.1–9.3 Mw Indian Ocean earthquake results in one of the largest tsunamis in recorded history, killing 280,000 people. Amidst this wreckage – geopolitical and natural – four epistemological shifts occur: Google releases Gmail; students create Facebook from their Harvard dorm rooms; the EU adds ten member states from Central and Eastern Europe; and, in the summer, republican delegates meet in New York City to nominate George W. Bush for re-election as president of the United States. In the shadow of these events, two women – protagonists in Hayes's *After Before* – hit the streets of NYC to randomly interview people about the upcoming presidential election. "Are you prepared for November 2?" they ask. Or alternately, "Are you prepared for November 3?" which receives quizzical reactions. As Hayes pointed out at the time, her quasi-fictional, quasi-documentary work was motivated by neither a desire to "document" that moment nor the promise of "truth-telling." That would be *cinéma-vérité*. Rather, Hayes set out to be an interloper in the media's homogenous representation of communal voices into a simple polemic of left versus right. Predicated on the realization that communities are in fact rhizomatic and contradictory, it wasn't a *lost* community Hayes was searching for, but a *contingent* one, present amidst all this historic noise.

In a way, it's true. Since *After Before* provides a snapshot of "New Yorkers" at the precipice of a sea change, it does activate historical desire. But what it piques is a longing for a *present*, an entirely different lack – not an actual loss – grammatically echoed by the film's title and mode of production. Shot two months before the November elections, Hayes knew her multi-channel installation would open in May of 2005, well after the results were tallied and the new president inaugurated. As an artwork, then, the film simultaneously denotes two temporalities: the *after* and the *before* of the electoral event haunting it. Which is to say, the artwork falls into the infinite regress of what Freud called *deferred action*, wherein the present tense can only ever be anticipated in advance, or read through hindsight. This psychoanalytic formulation challenges the classic Aristotelian model of time, the latter of which structures conventional documentary narrative and, correspondingly, the communal histories they set out to represent. For Aristotle, time marks change by our distinguishing between a "before" and an "after" in relation to a given event. The "now," on the other hand, stands outside of time because when we feel we are *in* time, we position ourselves somewhere along the linear succession of "befores" and "afters." Put another way, in the "now" *no time seems to have passed*. It is frozen. But when we perceive of a "before" and an "after," then we are speaking of time. Aristotelian subjects of time thus come *to be* on the perceived loss of what came *before* them in the current moment. But Hayes wants it both ways. Her subjects – of film, history and community – both *speak of* and *exist in* time, hence *collapsing* the documentarian's golden rule of sequential "befores" and "afters." Instead, we experience a regression into endlessly divisible "nows," an infinite *presence* of time looping past into present, present into past.

Still, a past horizon haunts *After Before*. In 1960s Europe, experimental filmmakers conducted on-the-street interviews to gauge a given community's desire – *Are you happy?* – amidst epistemological shifts in national, racial and sexual politics. In Paris, there was Jean Rouch and Edgar Morin's *Chronique d'un été* (1961), followed by Chris Marker's *Le Joli Mai* (1962). The former was "made without actors, but lived by men and women who devoted some of their time to a novel experiment of *film truth*," according to the directors, while in the latter Simone Signoret muses that "one would like to travel back to Paris after a long absence to find out whether the same keys open the same doors." By 1962, France had signed the Évian Accords, a prequel to ending The Algerian War for Independence, though backlashes were imminent, evidenced by one event echoing throughout *Le Joli Mai*: The Charonne Massacre, in which police brutality resulted in the deaths of 8 union and communist members protesting the bombings of Algerian and French citizens by the far-right paramilitary group *Organisation de l'armée secréte*. Looking at Marker's Paris today – in the wake of similar attacks by ISIS – perhaps the same keys *do* open the same doors. If so, it's another case of *before* collapsing with *after*, when dialectical, progressive change stands frozen in its tracks. An engineer in *Le Joli Mai* puts it this way: "For most people, the future is a bit like the horizon, you never reach it. It takes 30 years to get there, then 30 years more […]. An amazing thing is happening, the future has a lead on us." Hence the *other* horizon that lay behind us: the avant-garde desire to *capture* life in order to change it, an idyllic union of art and politics first anticipated by the historical Soviet avant-garde. But this horizon is one that Marker and company could never quite reach, and one to which Hayes and her contemporaries can never quite return.

While *After Before* retains *aspects* of her predecessors' experimental tactics, Hayes eschews any notion of "community" at the limit of infinitely retreating horizon lines, both past and future. Evoking Nancy again, I would say *After Before* instead locates its "community" in the *repressed* gap between infinite pairs of *parallax* lines. Two aspects of parallax vision are important to consider here. First, parallax vision constructs an *apparent* difference of an object's position when viewed from two different lines of sight. Secondly, objects to which we are closer always appear more peripatetic than do objects in the distance. Metaphorically speaking, that "object" can stand for an event, an identity, a concept or a community within range of our historical (distant) or contemporary (close) point-of-view. It follows, then, that communities viewed from a *critical distance* – as either "lost" or "yet to be" – appear to *congeal* into one absolute body, one at which both nostalgic and futurist artists aim. But a community viewed at a very close range – from a space of *complicit proximity* – would appear to scatter about, hither and yon, just beyond our grasp. This is the parallax community that Pier Paolo Pasolini's *Comizi d'amore* captured in 1964, another film reference for Hayes when conceiving of *After Before*. Employing the same interview format as Marker, Pasolini set out to *deconsecrate* a community of Catholic Italians unprepared to reconcile their so-called economic miracle (the future) with their pernicious medieval attitudes about sex (the past). This rabbit hole of *non-presence* – a libidinal lacuna subtending two paternal lines of vision, one catholic, the other capitalist – was one Pasolini willfully jumped into, in an effort to prove a point. When looked at from close range, his Italian "community" was in fact what George Bataille would have called *formless*. It's the same rabbit hole Hayes followed in shooting *After Before*, and today it's a portal to understanding what's still at stake in watching the film, *after* all is said and done.

Fast forward to 2016.

It's President Barack Hussein Obama's last days in office, and the cultural landscape is a labyrinth of polemical politics. The sovereign subject – that sacred object of all communities – bounces about on this field, to and fro, between various parallaxes. But one polemic, amidst the others, stops time in its tracks. In response to Black Lives Matter – the civil disobedience collective formed in 2012 to protest the continuing wrongful deaths of African Americans at the hands of a militarized U.S. police force –, a white nationalist group forms White Lives Matter, which the Southern Poverty Law Center swiftly declares a hate group. This is the *proximate* point-of-view from which I see (again) a poignant moment in *After Before*. A series of primal scenes rush forward from the interviewees when the interviewers ask: "What is the first political image you remember?" One answer – *The image of my 6th grade teacher in 1954 telling me to remember this time because it was the time of Brown vs. The Board of Education* – evokes a horizon behind us. But another response by a young black man – *I've been watching political views my whole life... me, myself one day? I wish I could be president* – points to a horizon that still lay in front of them. Standing in front of *After Before* today, I simultaneously cast two lines of sight upon it: the historic perspective of the 50s/60s, which I retrospectively occupy to look *forward* to *After Before*, and the contemporary perspective of 2008–2016, which I currently occupy to look *back* upon it. As such, *After Before*'s multifaceted "community" shimmers its (non)presence before me, refracting like a jewel within the subtended lacuna between these two gazes – the past and the future – where the film continues *to do its work* on me. As I write these words, now, in the summer of 2016, I look back at *After Before* in anticipation of the forthcoming presidential election – one in which all the racial and sexual issues of the cultural revolution are right back on the table – and conclude: *That I know not how to name what awaits us is a sure sign that it awaits us.*

Aesthetics of an Untethered Past

I am terribly preoccupied with the task [of] communicating with others – with the youngest, first of all, but with those of my age as well.[15]
Hans-Georg Gadamer

My interior dialogue with Gadamer, with Gadamer himself, with Gadamer alive, still alive, if I dare say, will not have ceased since our meeting in Paris [...]. At the time, indeed, I had called for a certain 'interruption.' Far from signifying the failure of the dialogue such an interruption could become the condition of comprehension and understanding.[16]
Jacques Derrida

Overture

On February 5, 1988, two philosophers – Hans-Georg Gadamer and Jacques Derrida – convene at the University of Heidelberg in lecture hall 13 of the Neue Aula, a venue reserved only for very special events.[17] It is one year before the fall of the Berlin Wall and seven years after the two philosophers had rendezvoused on a different stage in Paris to debate their indebtedness to Heidegger's notion of Being. But on that particular night, in Heidelberg, they meet to discuss the primal scene haunting the very amphitheater in which they sit: Heidegger's "The University and the Third Reich" speech, which he'd delivered there as rector of the University of Freiburg and a member of the Nazi Party in 1933. As a means of working through the ill deeds of their paternal figure, Derrida and Gadamer are asked to address how Heidegger's thought might causally be connected to his atrocious political affiliation. Spanning several days, the conversation is improvisational, at times even polemical, producing an unintended supplement to the event. The question becomes: how might we be "in time" with historical events as they return, Gadamer asked. How could we ever be "in time" with historical events given their meaning's endless deferral, Derrida counters. For Gadamer, our communal relation to the past is never absolute, but the caesura between the "then" and the "now" of historical events can be hinged through poetic experience. While for Derrida, we can never pick up where someone else left off. Any sense of our communing with a past event – poetic or otherwise – only represses the paradox of our Being in language. Hence the heated debate that filled the packed amphitheater in Heidelberg on February 5, 1988.

Having said that, what if both impulses – to commune and to disrupt – were at work in our conscious/unconscious experience of the past? Ultimately, this was Derrida's conclusion in another speech delivered in Heidelberg on February

15, 2003. Entitled "Uninterrupted Dialogue – Between Two Infinites, the Poem," it was in homage to Gadamer's passing. For in this moment – one embodied by a Paul Celan poem re-iterated by Derrida's eulogy – the two philosophers' perspectives came to mirror one another, producing a performative aesthetics of hinging an untethered past onto the present. In the case of the Gadamer-Derrida scenario, this entailed the writer-philosopher activating an historical poem. But should we reverse this formula, we might ask: what would it look like for a contemporary artist to poetically activate an historical event?

That Smallest Unit of History

Mary Kelly's *The Practical Past* – a collection of "lint works" she exhibited at Michell-Innes and Nash in 2017 – returns to us a constellation of events, near and far, gravitating around the political, primal scene colloquially known as *La pensée de 1968*. Her exhibition title derives from Hayden White's new historicist book of the same name, wherein he argues that all history is "anti-history, always written 'against' as well as on behalf of the (official) 'truth.'"[18] By this, White is getting at something quite similar to what the Gadamer-Derrida encounter enacted: that our consciousness of the "historical past" – the official account of an event based upon third person forensics – is understood through our experience of a "practical past" – that situational account related to our everyday personal lives.[19] In Kelly's constellation, there's first the meta-narrative of history, in which the year 1968 is the barycenter for 1940 and 2011. In each case, Kelly has compressed into lint an emblematic event immured within the field of photojournalism. Hence the image of Holland House Library after the London Blitz, the image of Paris in May before the general strike, and an Internet image of Tahrir Square during the Arab Spring. But that is not all. In reference to this trilogy of images are three small, metered texts, evoking both the practical past of which White speaks and the poetic hinge evoked by Derrida and Gadamer.

Which brings us to the lyrical thread connecting the overall trilogy. In each of these metered texts, Kelly establishes an historical *mise-en-scène* in the form of a second-person address – *You are here* – that places, or *sutures*, the reader into the transformed photograph/event. Each text then proceeds to evoke the larger historical milieu through bits and pieces – collective memory traces – of the recorded event. Hence Pearl Harbor and Hiroshima, for 1940, Algerian workers and Kent State, for 1968, and cell phones and Wall of Martyrs for 2011, all of which function as what Joel Fineman called the "historeme," that smallest minimal unit of historiographic fact.[20] But one of Kelly's phrases, common to all the texts, rises above these historemes. A sentence at once time-full and time-less:

Behind you, the photographer seconds before the shutter clicks, immuring the moment not long before you were born.

If this phrase indeed "captions" Kelly's trilogy, it's not in the photojournalist sense of anchoring an image's meaning.[21] Rather, the phrase phenomenologically denotes a moment in which the subject of history and in history is photo-graphed, which is to say, the moment in which she/he is captured as the subject and brought into the picture of history. The phrase thus destabilizes any unitary historical meaning that the trilogy might otherwise signify, affording instead a maze of conflicting temporalities and identifications. Together the historemes and the phrase "Behind you…" hinge the lint works *between* the symbolic photographic referent that presents a *there-then* and our imaginary identification with it that refracts, like a jewel, in the *here-now*.

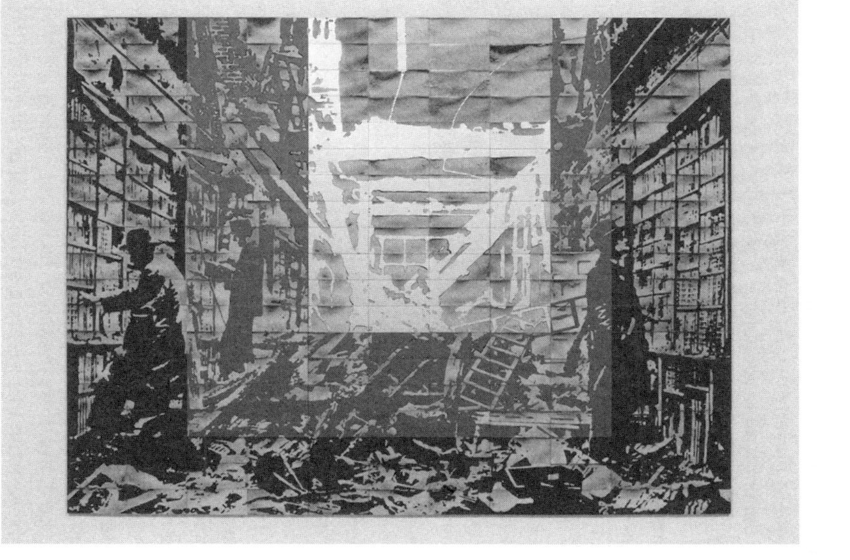

Mary Kelly, "Circa 1940." From: Circa Trilogy, 2004–16 (2015), compressed lint and projected light noise

The Task of Working Through

Kelly's performative engagement with psychoanalysis has always enabled her to "interrogate the interrogation," as she puts it. This entails triangulating her own subject position within the seemingly objective political and aesthetic propositions of her artwork. Accordingly, of those artworks we could describe as procedural – from Kelly's canonical *Post-Partum Document* to the first chapter of her lint series, *Mea Culpa* – the psychoanalytic concept of "working through" has been instrumental. On this, Freud famously said that patients in analysis don't remember their primal scene. Rather, they act out its truth through repetition. In 1995, Kelly cited this phenomenon in terms of her writing on past aesthetic and political positions with which she, among others, identified:

"I have come to view my 'writing' as a form of 'acting out', that is, as a transference of the past onto the present situation with its renewed fascination with conceptual art and feminism of the 1970s."[22]

Today, our fascination with 70s political ideology has intensified alongside our renewed fascination with revolution, both historic and contemporary. Which makes sense, given that "every image of the past that is not recognized by the present as one of its own concerns threatens to disappear irretrievably," as Walter Benjamin put it. History, it seems, is something in which we perpetually *invest*. And it, in turn, reliably yields us a *return*. Working through the past thus means working through what returns – as if by chance, almost *mechanically* – in the present. As a further means of "working through," what if we then extend the notion of *writing* texts *on* the past, that Kelly mentions, to that of *making* art *of* the past? How might this instance a continuation of Kelly's procedural works? Moreover, how might this further instance our figure of the *hinge*?

Back to *The Practical Past.*

To produce her images, Kelly used the lint trap of her household dryer as a ready-made mold, which meant that the casting process for each image required months of washing and drying some tens of thousands of pounds of laundry. First, Kelly began by reducing the given iconic photograph to a line drawing and then further broke that up into a grid. Each section of the gird, in turn, corresponded to the dimensions of her dryer's lint trap. By inserting vinyl graphics based on the drawing into the trap, Kelly produced a re-presentation of the historical photograph through the ready-made process of lint collection. The original image was then re-established by arranging the individual lint sections to form a single panel.

In the process of Kelly literally and figuratively working through these historical representations, we might ask, what remains of the past? In a word, it is lint. That smallest unit of washing – that non-substantive surplus of the filtering process – casts off a little piece of historical representation, worked through by the artist, in place of re-presenting the actual event. Moreover, should we think of the historical "event" in terms of something that one can't directly encounter, then it's meaningful that the bits and pieces of Kelly's historical referents – the photojournalistic image – are pressed into something as non-substantive as lint, through which a filtering process posits a symbolic yet enigmatic trace in the place *of* the (representable) event. In terms of "filtering" the lint trap can therefore be likened to what Freud called the preconscious, that which paradoxically produces something in the process of its effacement or censorship. And it is here that Kelly's procedural linting parallels what I've been calling historical hinging. The effect of which is that if something ultimately remains of history in Kelly's transformed lint images, it is that *far away so close* feeling, telling you that somehow, somewhere, you are *here*.

The Anecdotal Horizon

Another trilogy within *The Practical Past* makes an historical demand upon us. In *News from Home,* we encounter letters from friends culled from Kelly's personal archives, also compressed in lint. Through these handwritten notes, imbued with all the affective longing attending such letters, we lean back into the complexity of living as a feminist in the 70s via anecdotal history. From *Beirut 1970*, which deals with sexuality and monogamy, *London 1974* with communal living and motherhood, and *Tucson 1972* with economic survival during the Vietnam War, *News from Home* insists on puncturing – at the same time as it belongs to – the historical *grand récit* that Kelly's artworks call forth. And it is there that we encounter the 'real' surplus of history, in the guise of what Joel Fineman called the pulsative capacity of the anecdote, which "establishes an event as an event within and yet without the framing context of historical successivity."[23] The truth of historical consciousness, in the case of Kelly's *Practice Past*, thus creates a type of fused horizon between communicating subjectivities, in the space of a caesura – or temporal crease – wherein the subject and history can overlap without collapsing into a singular entity or unitary meaning.[24]

On this note, the anecdotal pulse beating through *The Practical Past* initiates a history that's more dialogical than dialectical. But the nature of cross-generational conversations is that they are always performed *in situ*, such that events never repeat in quite the same way or in the same place. This historical reciprocity existing between the present and the past can be thought of as two mirrors infinitely reflecting each other, which echoes the subject's reciprocity within the field of the other. Kelly's subject *of* and *in* history is thus anti-Cartesian, defined more by the phrase "We speak to each other therefore I am," than "I think therefore I am."[25] The past, with which we communicate, may speak through us in a myriad of uncanny ways – for Kelly, it is the photographic click that immures a moment *before* we were born. But if we can think we can cage this moment in – to stop it in its tracks – then rest assured, the moment will as inevitably fly away as it certainly will return to work on us. Such is the *fort-da* aspect of tethering an untethered past.

Schmitt, You and Me

Sovereign is he who decides on the exception.[26]
  Carl Schmitt

History is ripe to repeat when certain geopolitical pheno-mena are in alignment. Consider the latest constellation of events appearing to connect nineteen-thirties Germany with the present-day United States: mass frustration with a liberal free market, public contempt for congressional gridlock, the election of an unforeseen populist authoritarian sovereign, the establishment of a corporatist narrative and the banning of an outside enemy. But, as Heraclitus famously said, even when history repeats we never step in the same river twice, because repetition is no mere duplication. Rather, historical events – aesthetic, political and theoretical – are always hap-pening in the present, as if for the first time. From this per-spective, the sum total of past events haunting us now can no more be repressed as *gone* than they can be received as *here*. For those of us not happily aligned with this uncanny alignment, the present seems to hover in suspended animation – a temporal abyss – between a perceived historical origin and a desired political future. As Lenin famously asked, for completely different reasons, "What is to be done?" One possible answer: When historical constellations return, practitioners of critical aesthetics need to repeat more *conscientiously*. Which is to say, they need to "work through" the past, as Sigmund Freud put it, toward achieving a different end. Metaphorically, this entails a kind of filmic time travel, whereby a protagonist returns to a past event in a preemptive move, for example, to defuse a bomb that threatens to destroy the future.

Omar Mismar's film installation *Schmitt, You and Me* is one such endeavor at time travel. And the bomb? That would be Carl Schmitt's "friend-enemy" paradigm, the cornerstone of the German political theorist's "total" state. According to Schmitt, when an enemy enacts an existential threat to a nation, the sovereign authority has the legal power to impose a "state of exception," suspending the governing constitution and thus the law. Schmitt's worldview was formed in the nineteen-twenties Weimar Republic. Soon after, he became the "crown jurist" of the Third Reich, when the burning of the Reichstag in 1933 ushered in Hitler's perpetual state of exception. Even so, Schmitt's ideas appealed to more than just the Nazis. Select members of the Marxist Frankfurt School also found his ideas compelling. In 1930, Walter Benjamin wrote the jurist: "[Y]our mode of research in the realm of political philosophy has confirmed my own mode of research in matters concerning the philosophy of art."[27] And Schmitt's appeal doesn't end there. If something about Schmitt continues to stick, it might be the state of the exception's paradoxical status, what Giorgio Agamben calls its "being-outside, and yet belonging" topological structure.[28] As Schmitt put it: "[T]he sovereign stands outside of the normally valid

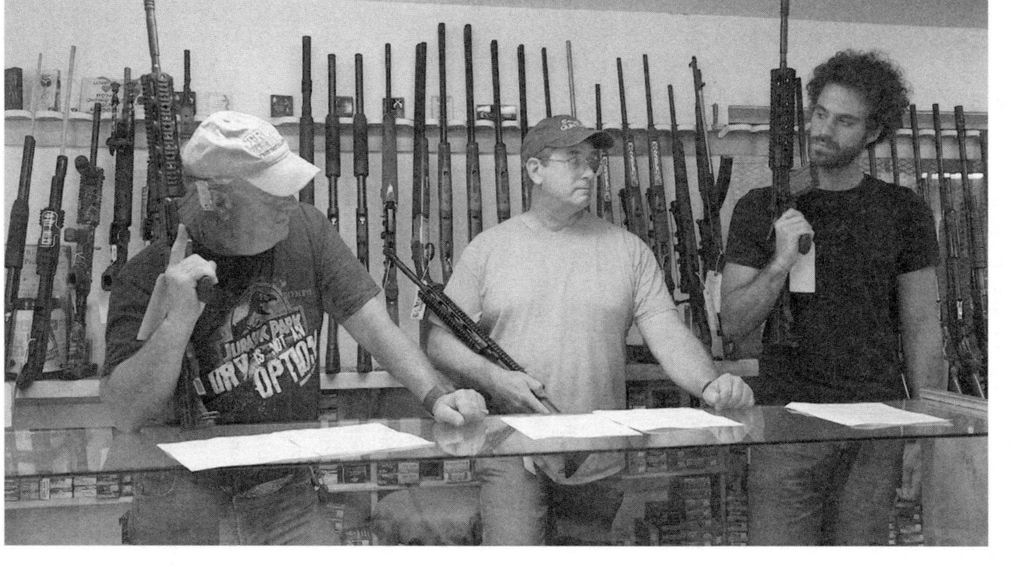

Omar Mismar, "Schmitt, You and Me," 2016-2017, video installation, 55' loop, video still

juridical order, and yet belongs to it, for it is he who is responsible for deciding whether the constitution can be suspended in toto."[29] This borderline status – the sovereign's indeterminate zone between law and anomie – similarly defines the enemy's relation to the friend. Although the enemy – that collective embodiment of the "not me" – appears to be outside the friend's milieu, the enemy is quintessential to the nation-state as its *raison d'être*. Annihilate your enemy and you annihilate yourself. Therein lies the bomb. Therein lies the reason Schmitt *sticks*.

The enemy is the embodiment of your own question.[30]

Schmitt, You and Me opens with an arresting shot. A middle-aged white man stands behind the counter of a gun shop, gazing silently into the camera. Framed by a row of rifles, he sports a baseball cap reading: "Trump Fence Building Co. Free Installation." As Roland Barthes would say, this description is the denotative meaning of the shot. Since the film was produced prior to the 2017 U.S. presidential election and exhibited after Donald J. Trump's inauguration as the 45th American president, this *mise-en-scène* stops time in its tracks. And when time is arrested, myth enters the picture. For this scaffolding of signifiers (*a white man in a gun shop wearing a Trump hat promoting a border wall*) is rife with political connotation. Evocative of Schmitt's friend-enemy paradigm, the man's political posture is clear: For America to be a great nation, one based upon the sacrosanct Second Amendment right to bear arms, a sovereign authority needs to secure her borders against the enemy. The film thus begins with a double-edged myth, one historical (Schmitt's *friend-enemy*), the other contemporary (Trump's *Make America Great Again*). Mismar, however, wedges an aesthetic proposition *between* these myths and defuses their explosive entanglement, which brings us to the film's backstory.

While residing in Skowhegan, Maine, Mismar frequented a local gun shop, hanging out with its owner Bruce and shop manager Bailey. After receiving a crash course in aiming and firing a gun at a shooting range, Mismar asked Bruce and Bailey if they would read excerpts from Carl Schmitt's 1932 text *The Concept of the Political* on camera in their shop. Flash forward to the film's establishing shot. Breaking the silence, Bruce reads from a paper held in hand: "The specific political distinction to which political actions and motives can be reduced is that between friend and enemy [...]. The political enemy is the other, the stranger; and it is sufficient for his nature that he is, in a specifically intense way, existentially something different and alien."

Throughout Mismar's film, Bruce and Bailey stammer and stutter through Schmitt's text. They read the more difficult passages over again or question the meaning of words they trip over: *atavistic, enmity, inimicus, hostis*. A couple of times they stop to read the text silently, Mismar beside them. In the course of working through the text, under the artist's stationary camera-eye, Bruce and Bailey *rehearse* Schmitt's words for a future, more perfect performance, which never arrives. The distinction between rehearsal and performance subsequently collapses, producing a filmic state of contingency – or *exception* – unmediated by Mismar's straightforward edits. Jean-Luc Godard created this kind of contingency by slowing down, stopping or speeding up his shots, producing an audiovisual "stutter" that interrupts the film's continuity. In *Schmitt, You and Me*, such interloping contingencies are not aesthetically staged. Rather, they're aesthetically put *on* stage. Curators Sabeth Buchmann, Ilse Lafer and Constanze Ruhm have recently argued that rehearsal-as-narrative appears "predominantly during periods of artistic-aesthetic and sociocultural transformations."[31] If so, then Mismar's rehearsal of Schmitt might be a response to the 24/7 digital *screen-of-consciousness* prevalent in art and politics today, in which bots, memes and YouTube reality shorts mythically buttress an existential threat that mimes Schmitt's friend-enemy paradigm. But this Internet enemy is reduced to stereotype, unlike the paradoxical version that *The Concept of the Political* performatively rehearses. For Schmitt, too, employed rhetorical starts, stops and repetitions in the writing of his text, through which his concept of the political ultimately *stutters* into ambiguity. This leaves Bruce and Bailey to ponder just where this allusive enemy is, in both the text and their real lives.

Which brings us to the absurdly sane idea of rehearsing Schmitt's friend-enemy paradigm in a gun shop. As Bailey notes up front: "I think what you want to know is how this all trickles down to people who want to buy guns for protection." This abstract question, performed *in situ*, presents two backdrops: one discursive (Schmitt), the other tangible (firearms), bound together by the qualia of phallic lure. For any abstract evocation of an "enemy" commands an equal and concrete presentation of a "shield." What else does the alpha male display of rifles represent but a *fascinum*, that ancient Roman amulet for a divinized phallus, a shield to ward off the enemy's "evil eye."[32] At the same time, the film's players display a general *lack* of expertise over Schmitt's enemy concept. What "trickles down" then is a "laying bare" of what lies at the core of the enemy-friend paradigm. And that "core" is the repressed fact that Schmitt's discursive shield − one meant to protect nations against an external, existential *presence* − more truthfully instances an internal, existential *lack* within the act of a "friend" calling out an "enemy." This "lack" is none other than the knowledge that behind the phallic mask of certitude, behind all our shields, lies nothing but our subjectivity tangled up with the Other. Bailey derives as much, when he pivots from discussing the psycho-dynamics of gun possession to that of waging war: "[It's] all subjective. What do *they* feel it is about *you* that makes them want to wage war? They believe they are right to everything they are doing." To which Bruce responds: "And, of course, we believe they are wrong." Having thus driven into the cul-de-sac of Schmitt's philosophical ambiguity, Bruce pauses before looking into the camera and asking: "Where do we go from here, Omar?"

The "state of exception" in which we live is not the exception but the rule.[33]

Flash back to 1945. The war is over. The American prosecutorial team at Nuremberg arrests Carl Schmitt as an "intellectual instigator," but he's hard to indict. Was the Reich's crown jurist legally culpable for Nazi persecutions at home and war crimes abroad? Or was he one of the most "eminent political writers of [his] time," whose analysis of Weimar's political structure might have led to its preservation, as Karl Lowenstein, Berlin advisor to the American prosecutors, countered.[34] Perhaps Schmitt was both, Lowenstein concluded. By 1936, Schmitt had fallen out with the SS, most likely because sympathizer-intellectuals were as dangerous to totalitarianism as the mob gangster.[35] He was an enemy of *both* Germany and the United States, and in his denouement, Schmitt was to become the exception *himself.* And yet, as his political capital waned, for some, his aesthetic-theoretical appeal persisted. As late as 1940, Benjamin abided by Schmitt's observation that the exception, which proved everything, was more interesting than the rule, with one caveat. Whereas Schmitt's sovereign authority transcended the very exception he declared, Benjamin's Baroque sovereign – put forth in his *Trauerspiel* – *transcended* his transcendence vis-à-vis his human flaws. Such double negation re-entered Benjamin's sovereign *back* into the world, the exception to the rule now becoming the rule. Samuel Weber interprets Benjamin's move thusly: "The otherness that is no longer allowed to remain transcendent therefore reappears this side of the horizon, represented as a cataract, abyss, or fall. Or even more radically, as allegory."[36]

Mismar and Benjamin are fellow travelers. The sovereign of *Schmitt, You and Me*, which is to say, its director, neither transcends the *mise-en-scène* nor is relegated to its margins. The world Mismar captures is, indeed, within his invisible camera eye, but he — the sovereign authority of the artwork — is simultaneously *caught* in the picture. Though we rarely see him, he's consistently on the side of the filmic horizon conventionally reserved for aesthetic illusion, as a kind of cataract in the gaze of directorial mastery. Sometimes, it is a small gesture, such as leaving in his first incorrect attempts at defining the words *inimicus* and *hostis*. Other times, it's awkwardness. Given Mismar's Lebanese heritage, his silent off-camera presence hovers over Bruce and Bailey's conversation about Middle Eastern "Holy Wars." But the sovereign-artist's exceptional presence as pure otherness — being outside but still belonging — is most powerfully felt through the film's allegorical impulse. Which is this: An artist (a stranger) enters a gun shop (an NRA lair). In the language of the culture wars, this is the quintessential friend-enemy situation. As I've laid out, however, Mismar's aesthetic process — that of cultural *encounter* — diffuses such a standoff. If it's true, as Schmitt said, that "the sovereign is he who decides the exception," then in Omar Mismar's art of encounter, the exception is always, in the end, the artist him- or herself.

Afterword: Myself as Another

Self-understanding is an interpretation; interpretation of the self, in turn, finds in the narrative, among other signs and symbols, a privileged form of mediation; the latter borrows from history as well as fiction, making a life story a fictional history or, if one prefers, a historical fiction, interweaving the historiographic style of biographies with the novelistic style of imaginary autobiographies.[37]
    Paul Ricœur

A specter haunts the pages of this volume, to whom I'll give the last word.

In Paul Ricœur's hermeneutical model we encounter a subject – manifest by way of personal identity – that's neither a self-sustaining *cogito* nor an alienated inchoate. Rather, Ricœur's subject is one that negotiates such polar tendencies as a kind of reconciliation under duress.[38] So how do we experience this aporic state? Cue Freud's theory of deferred action. In Ricœur's hands, personal identity is inextricably bound up with the subject's intuitive self-understanding as interpretation, which evolves us into embodying our "own story." That said, one's story is always a matter of a moebius back and forth, an inside out, consistent with Ricœur's theorization of narrative structure's double temporality, in which an experiential, descriptive sense of succession leads seamlessly into a retrospective, narrative sense of causality. Consequently, for the subject something that was unforeseeable was always already intuitively sensed as inevitable. For Ricœur, narrative – be it biographic or autobiographic, historical or literary – is the means by which we as subjects *experience* paradoxical time as simultaneously a contemporary moment, or pre-understanding of the world, and a retroactive moment of putting that world together into a kind of mythos, or aesthetic whole. Accordingly, narrative's perceived homogenous whole, a telos of sort, is only *relatively* autonomous vis-à-vis the heterogeneous world from which it derives.[39] This is because narrative is tethered to the world from which it comes, as well as to the world in which it is read, the way a dream inversely is tethered to consciousness, from which its individual signifying units come to us in sleep, and to the unconscious, from which our drives to reorganize those units originate. Keeping with the logic of the dreamwork as a metaphor for the artwork's hinge between the rational world and the energetic id, narrative structure "ambidextrously" points us to that which is knowable and differentiated, inasmuch as it leads us to the unconscious as a nondifferentiated energetic force field knowable only to *another*.

Were we to adapt Ricœur's hermeneutical model to the imbricated fields of art production and art writing, it would underscore the mirrored relationship between a given artwork and the writer addressing it vis-à-vis the world's pre-understanding that lies prior to them both. In which case, Ricœur's triadic structure, wherein narrative hinges the world's description and its prescription – the symbolic and the imaginary realms in Lacanese – would analogously situate the artwork as the hinge between art production *in* the world and art writing *of* the world. Furthermore, we might then think of the critic's "other" as the artwork itself – the locus of the *writer's* meaning, him or herself as *another* – which would deflate the critic's hegemonic task of aesthetic adjudication that typifies the ubiquitous art magazine and/or museum publication. This analogy, moreover, does not grant the artwork "agency" in any traditional sense. Rather, it short-circuits the locus of the artwork's meaning *solely* in the persona of the artist from which the artwork arrives, a tenacious mythology underscoring a mutated branch of identity politics that returns the *cogito* of essentialism back to the artist. I'm referring to the so-called "who may speak for whom" scandals, which have recently embattled American contemporary artists as far ranging as Sam Durant, Dana Schutz and Jimmie Durham. This phenomenon, however, is not limited to the Americas nor to art production. Rather, this essentialist *cogito* is now a global phenomenon within both visual culture and the recurrence of ethno-nationalist populism in politics and governance. As an ideology, the essentialist *cogito* masks the heterogeneous nature of the world it purports to describe and represent. In an adapted Ricœurian model, to the contrary, the artist who performatively delivers the artwork into the world of tangible things, as that world's interpretant, has no more privilege over the artwork's meaning than does the critic who delivers it into the world of discursive formations, as the artwork's interpretant. In place of this double authorial hegemonic, a *dance* ensues between artwork and writing, stand-ins for the artist and critic who, themselves, are re-interpreted by the world they set out to prescribe.

As to the critic's side of this dance, when I engage myself in the world as another – as a narrative or artwork that retroactively writes my current heterogeneous story, paradoxically, by way of my yet unknown, unrealized future homogeneous account of it – I must employ an intuitive sensitivity to the demand that artworks make upon me, in lieu of any programmatic compliance with the already written, the already made, the already known. It is, as Hannah Arendt wrote, to think of my position in the world as a contingent becoming *within* – and undoing *of* – the known world.[40] This is a tactic of production perhaps even more imperative now than it was in Arendt's time, given the current global empire in which center and margin, self and other, autobiography and biography, history and fiction, world and nation are intricately entangled within a seeming political dystopia. Even more specifically, when I intuit myself in a given moment in space-time – currently that is Beirut, the city in which these words are formulated and delivered – I apprehend my own story from the sense of a prospective anterior future, *what will have been* when I no longer reside where I am. For at the level of my quotidian experience of Beirut – a state of discordant concordance, a chiastic sea of alienation and certitude – my story is *just on the tip of my tongue*, awaiting to be told in the future as some unifying narrative by (or to) another person. But perhaps, paradoxically, that future other is always already *me*, in the here and now. In fact, discordantly, I'm quite certain that it is. And so it goes, back and forth. Not just in time – between the present and the future – but between myself and another, always in both places at once, such that the distance between these two perspectives is consecutively cut in half, endlessly divisible, as in Zeno's famed paradox. From this self-imposed crisis of *cogito*, I need the other to sustain myself. To annihilate the other is thus akin to self-immolation. Therein lies the *opening* for an ethics of myself as another.

Endnotes

1   This title is an homage to Jacques Derrida's own homage to Hans-Georg Gadamer, entitled: "Rams. Uninterrupted Dialogue – Between Two Infinities, the Poem," published in: Jacques Derrida, *Sovereignties in Question. The Poetics of Paul Celan*, eds. Thomas Dutoit and Outi Pasanen, New York 2005, 135–163.

2   Hans-Georg Gadamer, "Aesthetics and Hermeneutics," in: *The Gadamer Reader: A Bouquet of the Later Writings*, ed. Richard E. Palmer, Evanston 2007, 123–131, 123.

3   John Rajchman, "The Postmodern Museum," in: *Art in America*, October 1985, 110–117.

4   The phrase "subject of capitalism" is self-reflexive, denoting the subject that *is* capitalism as well as the subject that is produced *by* capitalism.

5   Jean-François Lyotard, *The Postmodern Condition: A Report on Knowledge*, Minneapolis 1984, 72. Written in 1979, it is notable that the book was translated into English in 1984, when Lyotard was curating *Les Immatériaux*.

6   Jean Francois Lyotard, *Vogue*, June – July 1985, cited in: Rajchman, "The Postmodern Museum."

7   John Rajchman, "*Les Immatériaux* Or How to Construct the History of Exhibitions," in: *Tate Papers*, No. 12, Autumn 2009, https://www.tate.org.uk/research/publications/tate-papers/12/les-immateriaux-or-how-to-construct-the-history-of-exhibitions.

8   Juli Carson, "Curating as a Verb: 100 Years of Nation-States," in: Brad Buckley, John Conomos (eds.), *A Companion to Curation*, Hoboken 2019, 57 (in print).

9   Jacques Derrida, Hans-Georg Gadamer, Philippe Lacoue-Labarthe, *Heidegger, Philosophy, and Politics: The Heidelberg Conference*, ed. Mireille Calle-Gruber,

trans. Jeff Fort, foreword Jean-Luc Nancy, New York 2016, xi.

10 Philippe Julien, *Jacques Lacan's Return to Freud: The Real, the Symbolic, and the Imaginary*, trans. Devra Beck Simiu, New York 1994, 80.

11 Sigmund Freud, "Remembering, Repeating, Working Through (Further Recommendations on the Technique of Psycho-Analysis II)," in: James Strachey (ed.), *The Standard Edition of the Complete Psychological Works of Sigmund Freud*, Vol. XII, London 1958, 147–156, 151.

12 Jean-Luc Nancy, *The Inoperative Community*, Minneapolis 1991, 8.

13 Rajchman, "The Postmodern Museum".

14 Nancy, *Inoperative Community*, 12.

15 Derrida, *Heidegger, Philosophy, and Politics*, 8.

16 Derrida, "Rams. Uninterrupted Dialogue – Between Two Infinities, the Poem," 139.

17 Reiner Wiehl, "Preface," in: Derrida, *Heidegger, Philosophy, and Politics*, pp. xi–xii.

18 Hayden White, *The Practical Past*, Evanston 2014, 6.

19 White, *Practical Past*, 9. The political philosopher Michael Oakeshott originally coined the term "practical past". White's appropriation of the term, to which Kelly returns, is decidedly more deconstructive than Oakeshott's definition.

20 Joel Fineman, "The History of the Anecdote: Fiction and Fiction," in: *The Subjectivity Effect in Western Literary Tradition: Essays Toward the Release of Shakespeare's Will*, Cambridge 1991, 59–87, 67.

21 In "The Photographic Message," Roland Barthes elucidates the photojournalistic convention whereby the text that attends the image constitutes "a parasitic message" on that image. In such case, "the image no longer *illustrates* the words; it is now the words which, structurally are parasitic on the image." Consequently, the text ends

up sublimating or rationalizing the image. See: Roland Barthes, *Image, Music, Text*, New York 1988, 25.

22 Mary Kelly, "Introduction: Remembering, Repeating, and Working-Through," in: *Mary Kelly, Imaging Desire*, Cambridge 1996, xv–xxix, xv.

23 Fineman, "The History of the Anecdote: Fiction and Fiction," 61.

24 For more on the notion of historical horizons and communicating subjectivities, see: Angelika Rauch-Rapaport, "Gadamer Needs Lacan: Gadamer's Approach to Tradition," in: *Journal of the British Society for Phenomenology*, Vol. 34, No. 3, Oct 2003, 309–326.

25 I'm appropriating Gadamer's notion of a "fusion of horizons" to *bend* White's version of the practical past towards the more psychoanalytic context of Kelly's work. On this front, see: P. Christopher Smith, who expounded upon Gadamer's fusion of horizons concept this way: "[…] conversation with others in the community is prior to, and determinative of any conversation of the self with itself. *Loquimur ergo sum,* not *cogito ergo sum* […]." See: P. Christopher Smith, "*Destruktion-Konstruktion:* Heidegger, Gadamer, Ricœur," in: Francis J. Mootz III, George H. Taylor (eds.), *Gadamer and Ricœur: Critical Horizons for Contemporary Hermeneutics*, New York 2011, 15–39, 16.

26 Carl Schmitt, *Political Theology: Four Chapters on the Concept of Sovereignty*, Chicago 1992, 5.

27 Horst Bredekamp, "Walter Benjamin's Esteem for Carl Schmitt," in: Jens Meierhenrich, Oliver Simons (ed.), *The Oxford Handbook of Carl Schmitt*, New York 2016, 679–704, 679.

28 Giorgio Agamben, *State of Exception*, Chicago 2005, 35.

29 Carl Schmitt, cited in: Agamben, *State of Exception*, 35.

30 Carl Schmitt, "Ex Captivitate Salus" (1947), cited in: Bredekamp, "Walter Benjamin's Esteem for Carl

Schmitt," 682. Also cited by Jacob Taubes, *To Carl Schmitt: Letters and Reflections*, New York 2013, 37.

31 Sabeth Buchmann, Ilse Lafer, Constanze Ruhm, *Putting Rehearsals to the Test: Practices of Rehearsal in Fine Arts, Film, Theatre, Theory, and Politics*, Vienna 2016, 14.

32 Jacques Lacan, *The Four Fundamental Concepts of Psycho-Analysis*, New York 1981, 118.

33 Walter Benjamin, cited in: Bredekamp, "Walter Benjamin's Esteem for Carl Schmitt," 686.

34 Joseph W. Bendersky, "Carl Schmitt's Path to Nuremberg: A Sixty-Year Reassessment," in: *Telos* 139, Summer 2007, 6–34, 16.

35 Hannah Arendt, *The Origins of Totalitarianism*, New York 1976, 339.

36 Samuel Weber, *Benjamin's Abilities*, Cambridge 2008, 187.

37 Paul Ricœur, *Oneself as Another*, trans. Kathleen Blamey, Chicago 1992, 114.

38 I've appropriated Theodor Adorno's phrase "reconciliation under duress" as a means of signaling a certain convergence between Ricœur's notion of double temporality and Adorno's notion of negative dialectics.

39 For a more thorough explication of Ricœur's theory of the narrator's "emplotment" within narrative structure and the manner in which "double temporality" determines both literary voice and subject matter, see: William C. Dowling, *Ricœur on Time and Narrative*, Notre Dame 2011.

40 Hannah Arendt, "Thinking and Moral Considerations" (1971), in: *Responsibility and Judgment*, ed. Jerome Kohn, New York 2003, 159-189.

Looking Back:
That Obscure Object of Gender

As part of her contribution to the 2010 Whitney Biennial, Kerry Tribe restaged Hollis Frampton's 1971 film *Critical Mass* as a live performance.[1] And with this gesture of repetition, the question of the gaze – a keystone concept of gender and film studies since the early 1980s – once again entered the picture. And yet, Tribe's *Critical Mass* provided an anamorphic twist on the subject of the gaze. To best understand how this happens, we must first set the scene.

Ever since Barbara Kruger's iconic image *Your Gaze Hits the Side of My Face* interrogated the ubiquity of female imagery in discourse – what Laura Mulvey proscribed as that object given-to-be-seen – a polemic among feminists ensued. Does one re-situate the female image, a la Cindy Sherman?[2] Or simply discard it, a la Mary Kelly?"[3] This comprises the so-called "male gaze" predicament – one based upon Jacques Lacan's notion of the Imaginary – put forth in the 1980s. Since then, a subsequent generation of artists – one informed by conceptualism and feminism – believe that gender positions can't be interrogated in their place, be it in pre-feminist or feminist contexts where "male" and "female" signs are presumed to be stable. Rather, when the question of subjectivity is addressed within a more permeable space – one bordering on the intangible – we more accurately glean (psychoanalytically) the gendered object: not an object *of* desire but an object *cause* of desire. Significantly, this (unfulfillable) desire entails the fantasy of being whole (again) in one's identity. This is the theory of the *formless* gaze – one based upon Lacan's notion of the Real – that another branch of feminists embraced in the 1990s. It is this notion of the gaze that surfaces in Kerry Tribe's version of *Critical Mass*. In advance of explicating how this happens in her work, a schematic philosophical etiology of the gaze is helpful.

"I saw myself seeing myself," are the words Lacan used to describe Jean-Paul Sartre's Cartesian notion of the gaze, one "by which the subject apprehends himself as thought." This describes the "bipolar reflexive position [...] by which as soon as I perceive, my representations belong to me."[4] In this configuration of the gaze, the looker is situated at the geometral point of Lacan's scheme, the object being transformed into a representation that the looker possesses and controls. In the real world, this is instanced both by the Camera Obscura (where the subject masters the image vis-à-vis the point of light) and Camera Lucida (where the subject masters the image vis-à-vis geometrical perspective). However, should the bearer-of-the-look lose control over his object, which is to say, if the possessive quality of the gaze is inverted, then the looker becomes embodied, transformed into an object within the field of the Other. For Sartre this was imagined through the sound of rustling leaves when he thought he was alone: "What I apprehend immediately when I hear the branches crackling behind me is not that *there is someone there*; it is that I am vulnerable, that I have a body

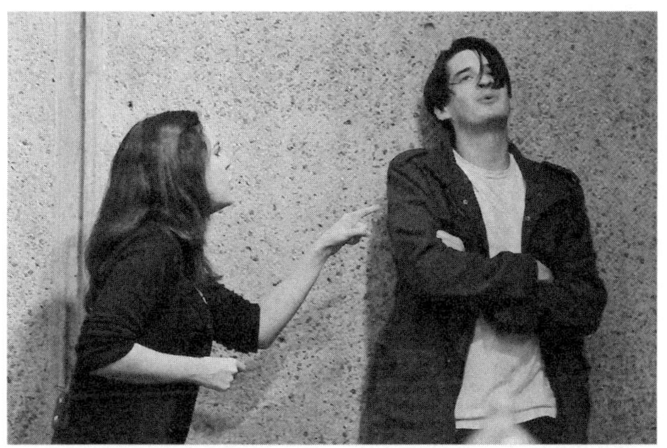

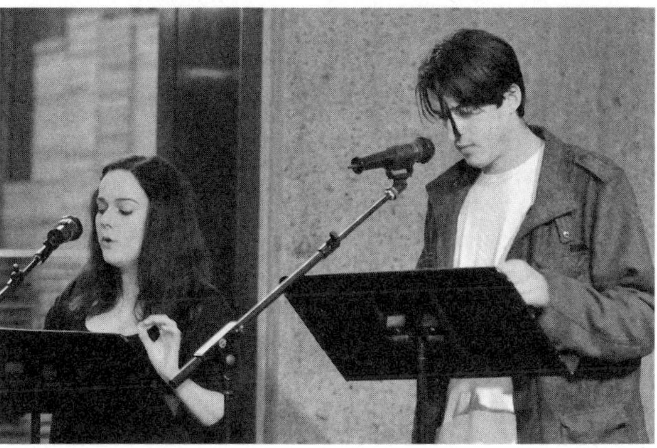

Images from Kerry Tribe's performative reading of Hollis Frampton's film *Critical Mass*, staged in conjunction with the 2010 Whitney Biennial. In each image, on left Jasmine Woods, on right Reed Windle

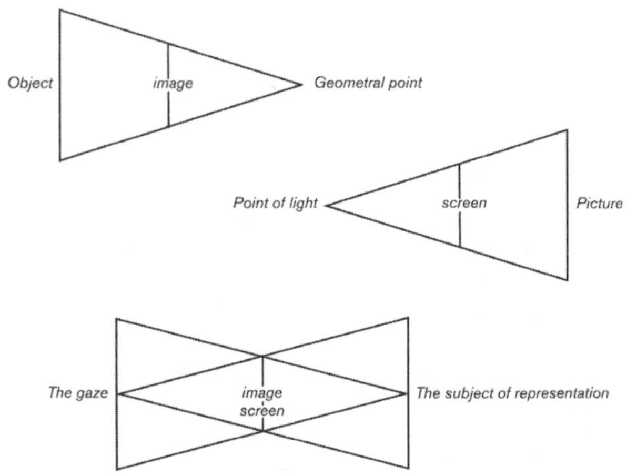

Lacanian Gaze Schema, 1973

which can be hurt, that I occupy a place and that I cannot in any case escape from the space in which I am without defense – in short, I *am seen*."[5]

Sartre's notion of the gaze is therefore a spatial one, a phenomenon previously described by René Descartes in his text *Dioptrique*. An illustration for a 1724 edition of Descartes' treatise displays a man, blindfolded, negotiating his way through a landscape with the aid of two sticks. Referring to this illustration, Denis Diderot remarked: "Neither Descartes nor those who followed him have been able to give a clearer conception of vision."[6] Simply, Descartes had provided the quintessential example of embodied sight by which even a non-seeing person could "see himself in space" along the primary axes of figure versus ground. This is what Laura Mulvey and Barbara Kruger were getting at through their Sartrean interpretation of a woman's objectification under the bearer-of-the-look, whereby: *Your gaze hits the side of my face*. Moreover, from this Cartesian perspective we see the origins of Sartre's perceived castration as he fell under

60

the gaze. Although, it is still crucial to point out, that in both cases – be it the Cartesian or the feminist case – the subject still apprehends itself as occupying a place, as vulnerable as he or she might perceive themselves to be within that place.

Subsequent to Mulvey's foundational notion of the male gaze – the definitive axiom of British film theory and gender studies – Joan Copjec pioneered another theory of the gaze, one centered around Lacan's notion of an *objet petit a*. Simply, the *objet a* is not an object, per se, but a *function*. It stands in for that phantasmatic or "impossible object" that the subject perceives as being primordially lost to him/her but which, in fact, can never be retrieved. The impossibility of the phantasmatic object's retrieval insures that the subject's drive remains active and his or her consciousness desirous. In the case of the scopic drive, it ensures that the subject continues to look "beyond" what he or she is given to see in the space of the image. Here is how Copjec differentiates the two notions of the gaze: "In film theory, the gaze is located 'in front of' the image [...]. The subject identifies and co-incides with the gaze. In Lacan, on the other hand, the gaze is located 'behind' the image, as that which fails to appear in it and thus as that which makes meaning suspect. And the subject, instead of coinciding with or identifying with the gaze, is rather cut off from it [...]. [Accordingly] when you encounter the gaze of the Other, you meet not a seeing eye but a blind one."[7]

In Copjec's scenario, the subject is thus neither in the position of the "looker" nor the "object" but elided between these two positions because, in this case, Cartesian sight fails. Simply, I do not see because I am *not seen*. And if meaning is suspect in this case, it is because one has fallen into the space of non-meaning, which Lacan's well-known Venn Diagram – published in *The Four Fundamental Concepts of Psychoanalysis* – posits as the space between pure being (the Subject) and pure meaning (the Other), i.e. between existence and representation. This experience of the gaze is

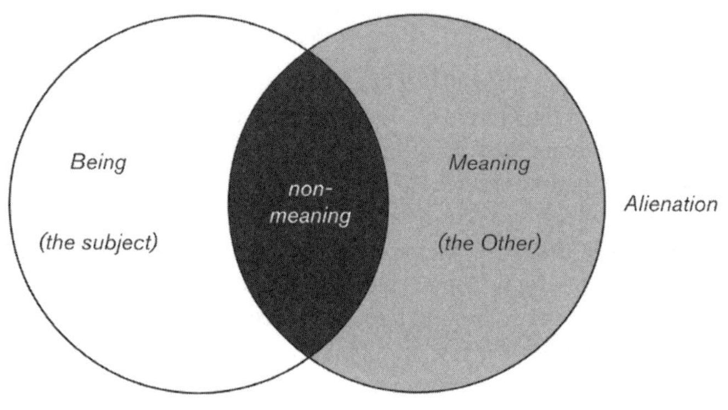

Lacanian Venn Diagram, 1973

underscored by Lacan's famed Gaze Diagram, wherein the Imaginary points of the "Camera Lucida" triangle (the geometral point) and the "Camera Obscura" triangle (the point of light) are imbricated, creating a space of elision, a space of non-sight. Consequently, an instance of non-meaning is produced because the concepts of self versus other – which is to say, the axes of figure versus ground – begin to fray. This is the gaze behind Lacan's famous anecdote recounted in Seminar XI, one that entailed his being at sea on a small fishing boat with the young fisherman Petit-Jean who mockingly pointed out to the good doctor: "You see that can [glimmering in the sun]? Do you see it? Well, it doesn't see you!" The point of this little story, Lacan explains, is that "at that moment [...]. [I] looked like nothing on earth. In short, I was rather out of place in the picture."[8]

Which brings us to the question of anamorphosis, the conceptual scaffolding of Kerry Tribe's reworking of Frampton's *Critical Mass*. In *The Ambassadors* of 1533 – the most famous example of the anamorphic object in the Western canon – Hans Holbein depicts two men surrounded by the trappings of a learned society, what Lacan would call subjects of the Symbolic register. In the lower part of the painting you'll see an elongated object slashing upward and to the right of the picture plane. Should we move to an oblique angle, the object is revealed to be a skull produced by the process of anamorphic perspective: i.e. *the representation of an image that is copied square-by-square into a distorted grid.* What's unique about Holbein's anamorphic object is that it is interjected onto – or flies across – the geometrical perspective that is the *Ambassadors'* Symbolic domain. Consequently, we can never see the learned men or the skull at once – one exists at the expense of the other. Against Durer's Camera Lucida configuration – whereby the viewing subject is squarely positioned in front of his object so that he might represent this object point-by-point as his possession – Holbein's *Ambassadors* invert the geometrical perspective so that what we have is not a restoration of the world onto the image but the *distortion* of it onto another surface. Moreover, the viewer can never see both points-of-view at once from one position. As such, this produces a "stretching out" of the representational world through which Symbolic meaning is challenged.

Indeed, if there's an equivalent anamorphic perspective to Tribe's *Critical Mass*, it can be located in the act of her stretching Frampton's film into a distorted one-to-one repetition of the original projection (then) onto a two-part performance (now). Accordingly, if you only see the Frampton film, you don't see the Tribe performance. But once you've seen the Tribe, you never quite see the Frampton again from the same perspective. Instead, the original film flies across Tribe's performance retroactively redefined.

But let's begin again.

Grammatically speaking, the object in Tribe's performance is Frampton's film, to which her actors direct their mimetic actions. In the original, a couple improvises a break-up, their argument reflecting the trials and tribulations of the sexual revolution. Frampton filmed the argument as a whole and then edited the footage into a series of stutters and repetitions, which is how the film exists today. In Tribe's redux, her performers reenact both aspects of Frampton's film, the working process and the final edit. In the first part of the performance, the audience witnesses a verbatim reenactment of the original argument that was improvised by Frampton's actors. In the second part, Tribe's performers reenact the film's dialogue, complete with the interruptions and stutters produced by Frampton's disruptive edits.

Now, if we were to posit Frampton's *Critical Mass* as the "distancing point" of Tribe's reenactment – that is, if Frampton's film is the historical point whereupon two imaginary parallel lines meet within a non-Euclidean universe – what we have, then, is an anamorphic re-presentation of 1970s avant-garde film (the object of art) vis-à-vis 1980s feminist politics (the object of gender) in the present. Moreover, if Tribe's performance stages an anamorphosis, it's because when we see Frampton's perspective – in the space of Tribe's performance – we first and foremost see an avant-garde critique of cinematic narrative in the guise of what Stan Brakhage called a "universal" work of art that "deals with all quarrels."[9]

This is Tribe's first operation, whereby the restaged argument is performed so naturalistically, in situ, that the Whitney audience at first mistakes the performance for a real quarrel: *Just another day in New York City.* Paradoxically, this cognitive misidentification entails a visceral identification on behalf of the audience with either party of the argument: *Oh yes I've been there before. That's me!* This is the "I see myself seeing myself" aspect of Tribe's performance, whereupon we encounter a Sartrean notion of the gaze latent in Frampton's film, even though his work was dedicated to casting *out* the specter of all such narrative haunting cinema.[10] And yet, in Tribe's hands, this universalist, identity-based aspect of the gaze is undone as soon as the performative nature of the couple's outburst is recognized, which is to say, as soon as the original *Critical Mass* re-enters Tribe's performative *mise-en-scène* as an anamorphic object.

This is Tribe's second operation. It is the moment that a paradoxical object arises in the performance. As surrogates for the subject caught and split within the language of his/her gender position, Tribe's actors – *given-to-be-seen* – are objects of the audience's simultaneous identification and dis-identification with a spectacle that is both real and re-constructed. Furthermore, if "we see ourselves seeing our-selves," it is in the aphasic moment between the subjects with whom we identified only moments ago. In this moment of great artificiality – one in which the cacophony of stutters and breaks exchanged by the performers signifies this event as a representation – the viewer's complete, embodied iden-tification with the event is elided. And instead of providing us with an object of gender, upon which we might gaze and with whom we might identify, Tribe's performance gives rise to an object *cause* of desire – an object at which we merely aim but cannot possess. For without a clear point of identifi-cation, the geometral gaze of sight is short-circuited, and, as a consequence, this representation fails "to belong to me."

To be sure, one way out of this scenario is for us to cast our Symbolic net back onto the avant-garde moment of Frampton's historical film, in which case the linguistic bra-vado of Tribe's performers can be visualized and embraced. From this perspective, we imagine how hard it would be for *us* to perform these lines, as *they* do, in public. But this move is merely another anamorphosis – a reaction-formation through which we may nostalgically suture our gaze back onto the conceptual avant-garde and feminist gender iden-tity as universal objects of desire – ones we can *see* and *possess*. The more critical viewing of Tribe's performance entails the suspension of any of polarities at hand – be it *then / now, real / fictive, self / other* – in place of a formless

hold out against all such petrified categorizations.[11] This happens when (and because) such play entails the elision of the
viewing subject's capacity to form universalist identifications,
at which point the more radical notion of the gaze – a blind
one from which we are cut off – momentarily arises.

Endnotes

1 It's important to note that Tribe's feminist return to *Critical Mass* was conceived for the Whitney Museum of Art. As such, there was a level of institutional reflexivity embedded in the event due to the site-specificity of Frampton's interdisciplinary practice, one based in the New York Avant-Garde art scene throughout the 1960s. Many modalities of Tribe's performance, which this essay explicates, underscore her critical, rather than nostalgic, notion of site-specificity. However, I thank Isabelle Graw for directing me to account further for the institutional aspect of Tribe's performance as performed at the Whiney Museum, in counter-distinction to its subsequent restaging at the Hammer Museum and LAXART in Los Angeles.

2 See Cindy Sherman's *Untitled Film Stills* (1977-1980), a series of photographic "self-portraits" in which the artist-woman is presented as a simulacrum.

3 See Mary Kelly's *Post-Partum Document* (1973-1979), a six-part series of altered ready-mades, in which the artist-mother is presented indexically rather than pictorially.

4 Jacques Lacan: *The Four Fundamental Concepts of Psychoanalysis*, New York 1973, 80.

5 Jean-Paul Sartre, *Being and Nothingness: An Essay on The Phenomenological Ontology*, New York 1956, 256.

6 Denis Diderot, "Lettres sur les aveugles," cited in Jonathan Crary, *Techniques of the Observer: On Vision and Modernity in the Nineteenth Century*, Cambridge 1992, 60.

7 Joan Copjec, *Read My Desire: Lacan Against the Historicists*, Cambridge 1994, 36.

8 Lacan, 95-96.

9 Stan Brakhage cited in *Circles of Confusion*, a five-screening series of films by Hollis Frampton (Part 2),

Los Angeles Filmforum, URL: https://www.brownpap-
ertickets.com/event/95580

10   Due to the tenaciousness of narrative within our psy-
che, Frampton argued that its return was inevitable
even in the most abstract film work. In "A Pentagram
for Conjuring Narrative," Frampton argues: "A specter is
haunting cinema: the specter of narrative. If that appari-
tion is an Angel, we must embrace it; and if it is the Devil,
then we must cast it out. But we cannot know what it
is until we have met it face to face." P. Adams Sitney,
Avant-Garde Film: A Reader of Theory and Criticism,
New York 1978, 181.

11   The anamorphic nature of temporality that's at stake in
reperforming *Critical Mass* should also be noted, whereby a simultaneous instance of a "then" and a "now" is
impossible to view from the same (psychic) position in
time. This is contrary to Hegel's notion of time, whereby
the present and the past are discrete moments that can
nevertheless be perceived, simultaneously, from one
contemporary position. The aforementioned psychoanalytic notion time – one based upon what Freud called
Nachträglichkeit or deferred action – would instance a
temporal anamorphosis, whereby the past and the present are completely imbricated even though they appear
to be discrete moments in time. In the subject's everyday life, the "past" unconsciously flies across the plane
of the "present" and vice versa. Tribe's *Critical Mass*, as
I have laid it out, attempts to make this latent operation
conscious for the viewing subject. I thank Pamela M.
Lee for asking me to tease out this aspect of anamorphosis in Tribe's work.

Bibliography

Giorgio Agamben, *State of Exception*, Chicago 2005.
Hannah Arendt, "Thinking and Moral Considerations".
    (1971), in: *Responsibility and Judgment*, ed. Jerome
    Kohn, New York 2003, 159–189.
Hannah Arendt, *The Origins of Totalitarianism*, New York
    1976.
Roland Barthes, *Image, Music, Text*, New York 1988.
Joseph W. Bendersky, "Carl Schmitt's Path to Nuremberg:
    A Sixty-Year Reassessment," in: *Telos* 139, Summer
    2007.
Horst Bredekamp, "Walter Benjamin's Esteem for Carl
    Schmitt," in: Jens Meierhenrich, Oliver Simons (ed.),
    The Oxford Handbook of Carl Schmitt, New York
    2016.
Sabeth Buchmann, Ilse Lafer, Constanze Ruhm, *Putting
    Rehearsals to the Test: Practices of Rehearsal in Fine
    Arts, Film, Theatre, Theory, and Politics*, Vienna 2016.
Brad Buckley, John Conomos (eds.), *A Companion to
    Curation*, Hoboken 2019.
Jacques Derrida, Hans-Georg Gadamer, Philippe Lacoue-
    Labarthe, *Heidegger, Philosophy, and Politics: The
    Heidelberg Conference*, ed. Mireille Calle-Gruber,
    trans. Jeff Fort, foreword Jean-Luc Nancy, New York
    2016.
Jacques Derrida, "Rams. Uninterrupted Dialogue –
    Between Two Infinities, the Poem," in: Jacques Derrida,
    Sovereignties in Question. The Poetics of Paul Celan,
    eds. Thomas Dutoit and Outi Pasanen, New York 2005.
William C. Dowling, *Ricœur on Time and Narrative*,
    Notre Dame 2011.
Joel Fineman, "The History of the Anecdote: Fiction
    and Fiction," in: *The Subjectivity Effect in Western
    Literary Tradition: Essays Toward the Release of
    Shakespeare's Will*, Cambridge 1991, 59–87, 67.

Sigmund Freud, "Remembering, Repeating, Working
    Through (Further Recommendations on the Technique
    of Psycho-Analysis II)," in: James Strachey (ed.),
    *The Standard Edition of the Complete Psychological
    Works of Sigmund Freud*, Vol. XII, London 1958.
Hans-Georg Gadamer, "Aesthetics and Hermeneutics,"
    in: *The Gadamer Reader: A Bouquet of the Later
    Writings*, ed. Richard E. Palmer, Evanston 2007.
Philippe Julien, *Jacques Lacan's Return to Freud: The Real,
    the Symbolic, and the Imaginary*, trans. Devra Beck
    Simiu, New York 1994.
Mary Kelly, "Introduction: Remembering, Repeating, and
    Working-Through," in: Mary Kelly, *Imaging Desire*,
    Cambridge 1996.
Jacques Lacan: *The Four Fundamental Concepts of
    Psychoanalysis*, New York, 1973.
Jean-François Lyotard, *The Postmodern Condition:
    A Report on Knowledge*, Minneapolis 1984.
Jean-Luc Nancy, *The Inoperative Community*, Minneapolis
    1991.
John Rajchman, "*Les Immatériaux* Or How to Construct the
    History of Exhibitions," in: *Tate Papers*, No. 12, Autumn
    2009, https://www.tate.org.uk/research/
    publications/tate-papers/12/les-immateriaux
    -or-how-to-construct-the-history-of-exhibitions.
John Rajchman, "The Postmodern Museum," in: *Art in
    America*, October 1985, 111–117.
Angelika Rauch-Rapaport, "Gadamer Needs Lacan:
    Gadamer's Approach to Tradition," in: *Journal of the
    British Society for Phenomenology*, Vol. 34, No. 3,
    October 2003, 309–326.
Paul Ricœur, *Oneself as Another*, trans. Kathleen Blamey,
    Chicago 1992.
Carl Schmitt, *Political Theology: Four Chapters on the
    Concept of Sovereignty*, Chicago 1992.